All THINGS SEAHORSES
For Kids

FILLED WITH PLENTY OF FACTS, PHOTOS, AND FUN TO LEARN ALL ABOUT SEAHORSES

ANIMAL READS

WWW.ANIMALREADS.COM

THIS BOOK BELONGS TO...

_____

_____

WWW.ANIMALREADS.COM

WHAT'S SWIMMING INSIDE?

Meet the Magical Seahorses! 1

Seahorses 5
   What are They, Exactly?

Characteristics & Appearance 11
   The Seahorse Super Features

Home Sweet Home 27
   Where in the World Are the Seahorses?

What's for Lunch? 35
   The Seahorses Diet

Meet Some of the Coolest
Members of the Seahorse Family 41

The Seahorse Lifecycle 55
   Growing Up Seahorse!

More Awesome Seahorse Trivia 67

You're a Seahorse Pro! 81

Thank You! 85

MEET THE MAGICAL SEAHORSES!

In the shallows of the deep blue ocean, where colorful corals thrive and fish frolic in mild currents, there lives a teeny-tiny creature with the head of a *horse*, the tail of a *monkey*, and the ability to change color *as if by magic*. Sounds like something out of a fairy tale, right?

Well, **meet the extraordinary seahorse!**

Seahorses are some of the quirkiest creatures living in the ocean. They might be small, but they are mighty and even a bit surprising.

Did you know, for example, that seahorses are terrible swimmers?

Isn't that astonishing, given they live in the sea?! There are many incredible facts to learn about seahorses, so why don't you join us on an exciting underwater adventure and meet them? Together, we will discover everything that makes seahorses special: from their unique body armor and head shape to their sneaky hunting tricks, twirly dance moves, and the fantastic way they can change color to avoid being eaten by bigger fish. We promise that you will be a real seahorse expert by the end!

So, grab your snorkel and flippers, and let's journey into the amazing, watery world of seahorses.

Let the adventure begin!

SEAHORSES
WHAT ARE THEY, EXACTLY?

Alright, budding marine biologist, let's start with the basics! *What exactly is a seahorse?*

A seahorse is a small fish that looks absolutely **nothing** like a fish.

The underwater world is famous for hosting some pretty weird-looking animals, but even among them, the seahorse takes the cake for being *the most extra*. Just between us, this little critter doesn't even look real!

Seahorses are known for having the head of a horse and a curly, twisty tail that resembles a monkey's. Instead of being covered in scales like most fish, a seahorse's body is covered in **bony plates** arranged in circles around their bodies. These plates make them look rigid and distinguished, like miniature knights in armor ready for battle!

Seahorses belong to a particular group of animals called **Syngnathidae** (pronounced "sin-GNATH-i-dee"). This group is like a big family, where all the members are a little different and unique yet have some traits in common — a little similar to a human family! Aside from seahorses, this family includes pipefish and seadragons, too.

You might be wondering why we group animals into families. Well, imagine you're building a giant puzzle with hundreds of pieces. To solve the puzzle, it helps to first sort pieces by color and similarities, right? Grouping animals with similar traits works much the same way. Scientists group animals based on their similarities, like their body structure, the way they eat, and how or where they live. This helps us understand which ones are related. Once we know which animals are related, we can learn more about them. For example, because seahorses are related to pipefish and seadragons, we know they might share similar behaviors and habitats. It's like having a big family tree that shows us how all these beautiful creatures are connected. It's like our big puzzle!

Large animal families are also often divided into smaller groups. In the case of the seahorse, this

smaller group is called **Hippocampus** (hip-uh-KAM-pus). Hippocampus means "sea horse" in Greek, which is pretty fitting considering their outlandish looks.

Did you know?

The word hippocampus is related to hippopotamus. Both words come from Greek, with hippocampus meaning "sea horse" and hippopotamus meaning "river horse"!

WHAT DO YOU CALL A SEAHORSE THAT LIKES TO BREAKDANCE?

A Hip-Hop Campus

CHARACTERISTICS & APPEARANCE —
THE SEAHORSE SUPER FEATURES

Seahorses have some rather wacky characteristics, from their interesting body shape to their ability to change color and a distinct *inability* to swim well.

Let's find out all about them!

HEAD

It's not hard to guess where seahorses got their name. Yes, they really do look like tiny horses living in the sea. Their head resembles a horse's, except they have a **long snout** that looks more like a small vacuum cleaner hose. *And that's precisely what it is!* The seahorse's snout is like a built-in straw and is perfect for sucking up tiny bits of food that drift by them.

Another remarkable fact about seahorses is that their heads are angled in a way that they can get very close to their prey without being detected. This allows them to sneak up on their food and catch it (*or suck it!*) by surprise.

Seahorses also have a special joint in their neck called a **coronet**. It acts like a spring, allowing them to "spring" their necks back and forth really quickly when they need to snap up prey. The coronet is a small crown-like structure unique to each seahorse, just like a human fingerprint!

TAIL

Seahorses have what are known as **prehensile tails**, which means they can use them to grab or hold onto things, just like monkeys do. Their tails are curly and can wrap around objects like seaweed, corals, and even other seahorses, helping them stay in place and avoid being swept away by strong ocean currents. As you can imagine, seahorses can easily be carried off by strong currents since they are so light, small, and rigid. So, think of their curly tail as a built-in safety belt, which they use to stay put!

BODY ARMOR

The body armor of a seahorse is extraordinary. As we have already learned, seahorses have bony plates all over their body, which act like armor suits, protecting them from predators like large fish, sea turtles, rays, crayfish, and even sea-diving birds like herons and egrets. The body armor makes them stiff, so they cannot swim horizontally like most other fish. Instead, they swim upright, moving their little fins and keeping balance with their tail.

The one great thing about having a stiff body is that it helps seahorses blend in with their environment, making it harder for predators to spot

Can you spot the Pygmy Seahorse?

them. They stand upright in the water and can hold on to seaweed — so they blend in and look like floating seaweed, too! Mind you, the real superpower that helps seahorses escape predators is their next unique trait: **camouflage.**

COLOR CHANGING

One of the most magical features of seahorses is their ability to change color. This remarkable ability

is called **color changing** or **camouflage** when it's used for hiding, and it's something several amazing animals can do. Octopuses, chameleons, and cuttlefish are masters of this skill too!

In the case of seahorses, they can change their color to match their surroundings — turning green near seaweed, brown near the sandy ocean floor, or even creating patterns like spots and stripes to blend in with coral reefs. *It's really like having an invisibility cloak!*

This little guy is blending in with the ocean floor!

Wouldn't it be neat to have a superpower that lets you be invisible whenever you need to hide? Now, that would be a great superpower — you would ALWAYS win at hide and seek!

Seahorses are incredibly talented at changing into all sorts of colors, including shades of yellow, orange, red, brown, and gray. Some seahorses can even show off vibrant colors like bright purples and blues, which they often do during their special courtship dances.

You see, seahorses don't just change color to hide — they also use their color-changing powers to "talk" to other seahorses and find mates!

This amazing transformation happens thanks to special cells in their skin called chromatophores — think of them like tiny paint boxes that can open and close to show different colors. Some seahorses can change their colors in just minutes, while others take a bit longer to get their new look just right. Either way, it's pretty impressive!

SWIMMING STYLE

One of the strangest things about seahorses is their upright swimming style. They use a tiny fin on their back called the **dorsal fin**, which flutters super-fast, like a hummingbird's wings. This fin can beat up to 70 times per second, which is incredibly fast!

Let's try something fun: flap your hands as fast as possible for five seconds... *Ready?* **GO!**

WOW! You're pretty quick, but a seahorse's fin moves even faster than that! Even with all this fin-flapping, though, seahorses are actually pretty slow swimmers.

Here's a funny way to think about how seahorses swim: imagine trying to move a skateboard forward only by waving a restaurant menu behind you. Not very easy, right? That's kind of what it's like being a seahorse! No wonder they get tired so quickly when swimming.

Did you know?

Sadly, seahorses have been known to die of exhaustion in very rough seas just trying to swim against the current! Life in the sea can be harsh on these little guys and gals.

To help them move around, seahorses have two more tiny fins near their heads, one on each side. These fins work just like the rudders on boats — they help seahorses turn and stay steady in the water. Having these extra fins lets them move very precisely, almost like they're tip-toeing through the ocean!

One of the coolest things seahorses can do is **hover** in the water, staying almost perfectly still. It's like they're floating in space! This special skill helps them hunt for food — they can slowly drift toward their next meal without scaring it away.

While other fish zoom around chasing their food, seahorses are more like sneaky underwater ninjas, quietly hovering until the perfect moment to catch their prey!

If you're ever lucky enough to see a seahorse swimming in calm water, you're in for a treat. The way they move is so graceful it looks like they're doing a slow, beautiful dance in the ocean.

PERSONALITY

Now, let's talk about the personalities of these amazing creatures. Seahorses are mostly **solitary** animals, which means they prefer to live alone rather than in groups. Unlike some fish that swim in big groups, called **schools** in the fish world, seahorses tend to keep to themselves.

Most days, you'll find a seahorse quietly hanging out by itself, using its amazing curly tail to hold onto seaweed or coral. But don't worry — seahorses aren't lonely! They're just peaceful creatures who enjoy their "me time."

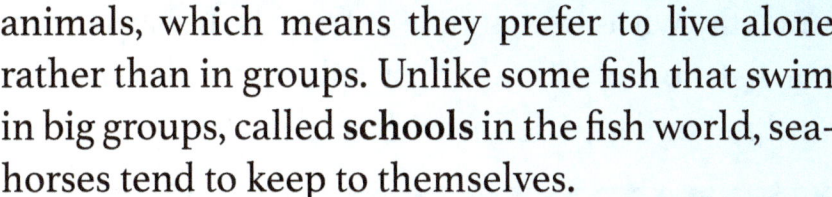

But here's where it gets really interesting! When it comes to finding a special someone, seahorses become the most romantic fish in the sea. They pick one partner (scientists call this being **monogamous**)

and stay with them like best friends. It's super rare for fish to do this — most fish just swim around and never settle down with one partner!

During mating season, these usually quiet creatures transform into underwater dancers! Seahorse couples perform beautiful courtship dances together, changing colors like underwater disco lights and wrapping their tails around each other. Imagine having a dance partner who could change colors while dancing — now that would be quite a show!

ALL THINGS SEAHORSES FOR KIDS 25

The most amazing part? Once seahorses find their perfect partner, they often stay together for the whole breeding season and sometimes even for their entire lives! That's like having a best friend forever but under the sea. This special bond makes seahorses stand out in the fish world, where most other fish never even remember who their partners were!

HOME SWEET HOME:
WHERE IN THE WORLD ARE THE SEAHORSES?

Now that we know what makes seahorses unique let's explore their **habitats**. Seahorses have some favorite hangouts in the ocean, but given their small and fragile size, they must carefully choose their homes.

What is a habitat? A habitat is just a fancy word for an animal's natural home. Think of how a lion lives in the grasslands of Africa or how a penguin lives in the icy Antarctic — those are their habitats!

Seahorses are pretty picky about where they live, and for good reason! Being small and not very strong swimmers, they need homes that offer both safety and plenty of food. Their favorite places to live are like underwater neighborhoods, and there are three main ones they love best:

Coral Reefs: Imagine the most colorful underwater city you can think of — that's a coral reef! These reefs are like busy apartment buildings made of coral, where seahorses can hide in all sorts of nooks and crannies. The best part? These reefs are packed with tiny sea creatures that seahorses love to eat.

Seagrass Beds: These are like underwater meadows with tall grass swaying in the currents. Seahorses love wrapping their tails around the seagrass stems, using them like nature's perfect anchor. The seagrass also attracts lots of small animals that seahorses enjoy snacking on.

Can you spot the seahorse hiding in the seagrass?

Mangroves: These special trees grow right in the water near coastlines, and their tangly roots create perfect hiding spots for seahorses. It's a perfect fortress to keep them safe!

All these homes have something in common — they're in shallow, warm waters near the coast. These areas are perfect for seahorses because the water is usually calm and peaceful, just the way they like it. The sunlight can easily reach the bottom in these shallow waters, which helps lots of plants grow.

These plants attract many tiny sea creatures that seahorses love to eat, and they also provide plenty of things for seahorses to grab onto with their special tails.

SEAHORSE SPOTS AROUND THE GLOBE

Let's take an imaginary trip around the world to visit some seahorse neighborhoods:

In the Atlantic Ocean (that's the big ocean between North and South America and Europe/Africa), you might find seahorses playing hide-and-seek along the coasts of:

- The United States, where they hide in seagrass near Florida's sunny shores

- Mexico's warm waters, where they dance among colorful coral reefs
- Brazil's tropical coastline, where they wrap their tails around mangrove roots

Swimming over to the Mediterranean Sea (the warm sea between Europe and Africa), seahorses hang out near the beautiful beaches of Greece, Italy, and Spain. Here, they love floating through underwater meadows of seagrass that wave gently in the current.

In the Indo-Pacific region (that's the huge area covering the Indian and Pacific Oceans), seahorses thrive in the crystal-clear waters around Indonesia, the Philippines, and Australia. These waters are like a gigantic underwater playground for seahorses, full of coral reefs and seagrass beds!

Finding a seahorse in the wild is like discovering buried treasure — it's super special and rare! Even experienced divers and snorkelers get excited when they spot one. That's because seahorses are mas-

ters of hiding, using their amazing camouflage powers to blend in with their surroundings. Plus, they're pretty shy and usually stay very still, making them look just like a piece of coral or seaweed!

Did you know?

Seahorses are very sensitive to climate change and habitat loss, which is when their favored environments, such as coral reefs and mangroves, are destroyed by overfishing, rising ocean temperatures, and an increase in destructive coastal storms. Protecting seahorses' marine habitat is essential to ensure their survival.

WHAT'S FOR LUNCH?
THE SEAHORSES DIET

Just like we need nutritious food to stay healthy and active, so does the seahorse. Wondering what these little creatures snack on?

Let's find out!

Seahorses are **carnivores**, which means they eat meat. Now, we know what you're thinking: a seahorse can't swim up to an underwater restaurant and order a steak! Instead, these clever creatures feast on something much smaller — tiny sea animals that are like living specks in the ocean.

But what can be even smaller than a seahorse, you ask? You'd be surprised! Their favorite foods are itty-bitty sea creatures called **copepods** and miniature shrimp. These tiny animals are part of a group called **plankton**, which are so small you'd need a microscope just to see them! Imagine creatures so tiny that thousands could fit on your fingernail — that's what seahorses love to eat!

A microscopic picture of copepods... a favorite meal of seahorses!

Here's something incredible: seahorses are like vacuum cleaners of the sea, constantly sucking up these tiny creatures with their snout. And when we say constantly, we mean it! Adult seahorses eat between 30 and 50 times every single day. That might sound like a lot, but wait until you hear about baby seahorses — they can gobble up to 3,000 tiny shrimp in just one day!

Want to know why seahorses eat so much? Here's their secret: **they don't have stomachs!** That's right — unlike us, seahorses have no storage space for their food. Everything they eat goes straight through their body, so they need to keep eating all day long. Imagine if you had no stomach — you'd have to eat breakfast, second breakfast, third breakfast, and keep going all day long just to stay full!

The way seahorses catch their food is pretty cool, too. They use their long snout like a built-in drinking straw, sucking up their tiny prey with a quick slurp. Even though they don't have any teeth, they make a funny clicking sound when they catch their

food — it sounds just like someone snapping their fingers or smacking their lips. *Click, click, slurp!*

Next time you're drinking a smoothie through a straw, think about the seahorse — you're eating just like they do! Though hopefully, you don't need to drink 30 smoothies a day like our hungry seahorse friends.

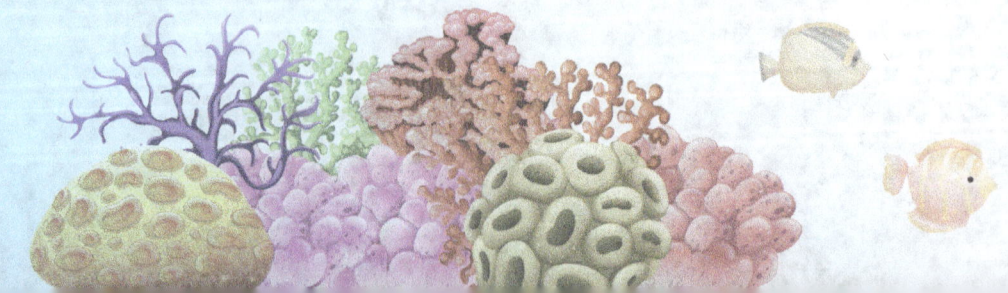

MEET SOME OF THE COOLEST MEMBERS OF THE SEAHORSE FAMILY

Do you feel like you're getting to know our adorable underwater sea monsters a little better? We hope so! Now might be an excellent time to dive a little deeper and meet some of the most fascinating members of the seahorse family.

There are around **46 known species of seahorses** in the world today, each with unique traits that make it stand out from the rest. While some are big and impressive, others are so tiny that you can't even see them!

Let's check out some of the most amazing species now!

COMMON SEAHORSE (HIPPOCAMPUS KUDA)

First up, we have the Common Seahorse. But don't let the name fool you — these seahorses are *anything* but ordinary!

The Common seahorse can vary in color from yellow to brown. They are also known as Spotted seahorses because some have stunning splashes of color throughout their body, just like polka dots. This species can grow up to 14 inches (35 cm) in length and is among the largest in the seahorse

 ALL THINGS SEAHORSES FOR KIDS 43

family. The spots can be in all sorts of colors, making each one look like a fantastic piece of living art. Found in countries like Indonesia, the Philippines, and Australia, the Common seahorse loves hanging out in seagrass beds, coral reefs, and mangrove swamps.

A common seahorse chilling under the sea

 Did you know?

Baby seahorses, called fry, are only the size of a grain of rice when they're born. Their skin is also transparent, and they are almost invisible.

LINED SEAHORSE (HIPPOCAMPUS ERECTUS)

Next, let's meet the Lined Seahorse, the "zebra" of the seahorse family. This species is known for having vertical stripes running along its entire body, which gives it a unique appearance. They can grow up to 12 inches (30 cm) and are found in the western Atlantic Ocean of North America, starting from Canada in the north and all the way south to Mexico and even further into Brazil. These seahorses can change into shades of yellow and brown, and

their stripes are particularly useful for blending into seagrass beds and coral reefs.

Did you know?

A seahorse lives in the ocean for 1-5 years. In an aquarium, however, seahorses can live up to seven years since they feed regularly and don't have to worry about predators. Be aware, though, that keeping seahorses in aquariums is a serious commitment, as they need specialized care and attention.

PYGMY SEAHORSE (HIPPOCAMPUS BARGIBANTI)

It's time to meet the Pygmy Seahorse. This tiny creature is under 1 inch (2 cm) long — which is way smaller than your thumb! What makes the Pygmy seahorse so special is its adorably small size *and* its unique, super bumpy texture. This little buddy is like a miniature, extra-armored underwater tank!

This minuscule seahorse is often found clinging to the sea fans and corals of Indonesia and the Philippines. It is so tiny that you would need a magnifying glass to see it properly, and that's not something one usually carries when snorkeling in trop-

ical seas, right? Aside from its ridiculously small size, the Pygmy seahorse also has bumps that stick out and change color, making it one of the best camouflage pros in the seahorse world. For all these reasons, it is the rarest seahorses to spot in the wild.

Can you spot the little Pygmy seahorse hidden here?

Did you know?

Seahorses can move their eyes independently of one another. So, one can look forward and the other backward at the same time! This essentially gives them a near 360-degree vision. Another nifty seahorse superpower to be impressed by!

DWARF SEAHORSE (HIPPOCAMPUS ZOSTERAE)

Closely related to the Pygmy is the Dwarf seahorse, which is only slightly bigger and grows to about 1 inch (2.5 cm) in length.

Mostly found in the Gulf of Mexico, these tiny seahorses are small but formidable. Their size makes them perfect for hiding among seagrasses, where they feed on tiny shrimp and copepods. Despite their size, they're tough little creatures, proving that you don't have to be big in size to be utterly amazing!

 ALL THINGS SEAHORSES FOR KIDS

Did you know?

Like most fish, seahorses do not look after their babies after birth, so the tiny specs of creatures must fend for themselves from the beginning. Since they are so small and are easily eaten by predators or carried into cold waters by currents, the survival rate of seahorse fry is less than 0.5%. That means only one in 200 newborn seahorses make it to adulthood!

BIG-BELLIED SEAHORSE (HIPPOCAMPUS ABDOMINALIS)

The couch potato of the seahorse world is the perfectly named the Big-bellied seahorse. With its big pot belly that makes it look like it's just feasted on a whole family-sized pizza, this big little guy is unique in the seahorse family. It is one of the largest species, growing to about 13-14 inches (35 cm) and one of the strongest. For these reasons, it thrives well in the strong currents off Australian and New Zealand coasts, where many smaller seahorses simply could not survive.

ALL THINGS SEAHORSES FOR KIDS | 51

Did you know?

The seahorse is one of just a handful of fish species in which the dad carries and gives birth to babies. The male seahorse carries the eggs in a special sac under its tail. The sac is called a **brood pouch,** and it can carry up to 2,000 babies at once!

LEAFY SEADRAGON (PHYCODURUS EQUES)

While not technically a seahorse, the Leafy Seadragon is a close relative, and we simply had to share it with you. With long, leaf-like appendages, the leafy seadragon looks like a beautiful piece of floating seaweed, which helps it blend seamlessly into its surroundings. Found along Australia's southern and eastern coasts, these dragons can grow up to 18 inches (45 cm) long.

While they might look ready for a fancy masquerade ball, these delicate-looking seadragons are pretty tough and capable hunters. They also have a tube-like mouth and can slurp *thousands* of shrimp-like creatures called **mysids** daily. They wait patiently for their prey to come close and then… slurp!

Another exciting feature of leafy seadragons is their tails. Unlike their seahorse cousins, they don't use their tails to hang onto seagrasses. Instead, they use them for balance and steering as they move through the water, just like a boat or plane might use its rudder. They also have almost transparent fins that they use to propel themselves forward. These "invisible" engines add to the illusion that they are just floating pieces of seaweed.

The impressive snout of a leafy seadragon

Did you know?

The seahorse family is huge and varied. While the smallest seahorse is barely bigger than your fingernail, some grow as long as a banana!

THE SEAHORSE LIFECYCLE
GROWING UP SEAHORSE!

Is it just us, or are seahorses some of the most interesting animals in the world? We indeed think so! So far, we have learned a little about how and where they live, what and how they eat, and the fantastic colors and sizes they come in. And now, it's time to learn more about the lifecycle of the seahorse — the journey from a teeny baby to a fully grown adult.

BIRTH AND EARLY LIFE

Seahorse babies, called **fry**, have an extraordinary beginning to life. Remember how we learned that male seahorses give birth? Here's how that happens.

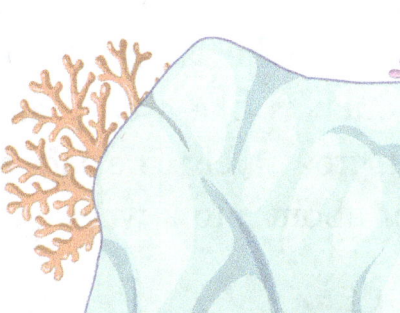

First, the mom seahorse places her eggs into a special pocket on the dad's belly called a **brood pouch**. This pouch is like a cozy apartment where the eggs can grow safely. The dad carries these precious eggs for about 2 to 4 weeks, keeping them warm and protected. When it's finally time for the babies to be born, something spectacular happens — the dad seahorse has strong muscle movements called **contractions** and out pop hundreds or even thousands of tiny baby seahorses! These babies are no bigger than a grain of rice and burst out into the ocean like confetti!

Once born, seahorse babies are fully independent. That means they don't need any help from their parents to survive. Well, they could do with *some* help, truth be told, but the natural world is tough sometimes, and seahorses must take care of themselves from the get-go.

The tiny babies must start finding food and hiding from predators immediately. It's a tough start, but seahorse fry are up for the challenge! Although they are small, fry already look like miniature versions of adult seahorses. Yet, they don't have the hard shell or ability to swim or hide very well. Still, you can certainly see the horse-shaped head and curly tail, except they are much more delicate than adults. During their early days, they stay near the water's surface, where they feed on tiny plankton. This stage can last a few weeks as they grow and start to look more and more like their parents.

ADOLESCENCE — THE TEEN YEARS

As the fry grow, they enter a stage called **adolescence.** Like human teenagers, young seahorses go through a period of quick growth. This stage typically lasts for several months, depending on the species. During this time, they learn essential skills like hunting for food and **camouflaging** to stay super safe. *Do you remember what camouflage means? We bet you do! It means blending into your environment and changing color so you can hide away from pesky predators.*

Adolescence is a tricky time for seahorses. They must be very careful and use all their hiding skills to avoid danger. But with each passing day, they get better at finding food and protecting themselves. As they grow, young seahorses move to deeper waters where they can find more food and better hiding places. Their bodies continue to develop, and they begin to show the characteristic features of adult seahorses, like their **prehensile tails** and **bony plates.**

ADULTHOOD — ALL GROWN UP

Seahorses reach adulthood when they are around six months to one year old. That's a little different from humans, right? The brand-new adult seahorse is now ready to find a mate and make a family. During **courtship**, when seahorses determine if they have found a suitable mate, they swim around one another and change colors to impress. To humans, it looks as if they are dancing in the water, often interlacing their tails to stay connected. They twirl and twist, showing off their charming moves.

It's like watching two underwater ballerinas perform a duet! This dance helps them bond and prepare for mating.

The "seahorse mating dance" is one of the most important ways seahorses communicate with one another. It may seem like it is simply a fun thing to do, but it is, in reality, the most essential way seahorses make friends and find mating partners.

Apart from romantic dances, seahorses have other ways to communicate. One way is by changing color or camouflaging. The tiny creatures use camouflage like we might do body language — "reading" someone's expression or stance to understand their feelings. Do you know how you can sometimes tell if an adult is happy or cross with you, even if they don't say anything? Well, it's very similar to that! Color changes are how seahorses "talk" to each other. For example, imagine you're a seahorse meeting your very best friend after a few days apart. Instead of saying "Hi!" you might turn bright purple or flash a crazy pattern to say, "Hey, it's me, I've missed you!" Seahorses also talk to each other through a series of clicking sounds. They are most likely to click when eating food and courting each other. We don't often think of fish making sounds, but many fish do. We just can't hear them! Seahorses not only click; they can also vibrate and growl when stressed or handled. As a dog growls, a seahorse might also growl to say, "Back off, buddy!"

Seahorse tail-holding is also like our human hand-holding. It is a way to bond, stay close, and ensure that one doesn't lose the other in a crowded coral reef!

Once paired, seahorses may stay together for several breeding cycles. A breeding cycle is when the female deposits eggs into the male's pouch until the fry are born. This can happen many times throughout their adult lives, ensuring they have plenty of opportunities to have offspring together.

THE CIRCLE OF SEAHORSE LIFE: LIFESPAN

As we've already learned, seahorses can live up to 1-5 years in the wild and a little longer if kept safely in an aquarium.

Just like how you need clean air, good food, and a safe home to stay healthy, seahorses need certain things to live a long and happy life. They thrive in crystal-clear, clean water at just the right temperature, with plenty of their favorite tiny foods to eat. They also need a peaceful home without too much stress and safe places to hide and rest.

 ALL THINGS SEAHORSES FOR KIDS   65

That is true both in the wild and in an aquarium.

Heads up!

You might be thinking, "Wow, seahorses are so cool — I want one as a pet!" But here's something important to know: seahorses need very special care, which makes them tricky to keep as pets. They need specific water conditions, big tanks, and specialized diet and care. A great place to see them up close is public aquariums, marine parks, and marine science centers, where experts make sure they are well cared for.

WHY DO SEAHORSES LIVE IN SALTWATER?

Because Pepper Water Makes Them Sneeze!

MORE AWESOME SEAHORSE TRIVIA

Woah, we have learned so much about sea horses already! Is your head spinning from all the amazing facts about these fantastic creatures?

Let's summarize the most important facts we have learned about seahorses and see if you still remember them all. We'll also add a few new awesome facts to keep you on your toes.

Ready? **Let's go!**

SEAHORSES ARE ONE OF THE FEW ANIMAL SPECIES WHERE THE MALES GIVE BIRTH.

Crazy, but true! Only a few animals share this incredible trait — the male carries and gives birth to young. A few fish and frog species do, but seahorses are perhaps most famous for showcasing this very unique trait. As you might remember, the female seahorse deposits eggs into the male's brood

pouch, which is similar to the pouch of a kangaroo. The "dad" then carries them for a few weeks until he's ready to release them. A few strong cramps and out they pop, in their hundreds and even thousands!

SEAHORSES ARE *SERIOUSLY* BAD SWIMMERS.

Luckily, seahorses have so many cool tricks up their sleeves to avoid being eaten by predators. Because if they had to rely on their swimming skills, oh dear! Seahorses are among the worst and slowest swimmers in the ocean and use their fins to bob up and down slowly rather than swim horizontally.

Yet they have a bunch of ways to evade predators, including camouflage, hovering, and anchoring to seaweed, sea plants, and coral reefs.

SEAHORSES USE THEIR TAILS TO HOLD STUFF.

Yes, they can hold on to seaweed, coral, marine plants, and one another with their tail. And that means that the largest seahorse could also hold your pinky finger. Awww!

ALL THINGS SEAHORSES FOR KIDS

SEAHORSES ARE ABSOLUTE MASTERS OF DISGUISE.

Using their camouflage ability as an invisibility cloak, seahorses can swiftly blend into their surroundings. Seaweed or seahorse? Rock or seahorse? Coral or seahorse? There's no way of knowing! This makes them the absolute masters of underwater disguises.

Ssshhhh... Don't tell anyone when you spot the seahorse

SEAHORSES DON'T ALL LOOK THE SAME.

Sure, they may *look* the same in body shape, but seahorses can vary a lot in size and external appearance. While some have spots or stripes, others have bumps and spikes. Every species has evolved to blend into its specific environment, so they look very different depending on where they live!

SEAHORSES CAN MOVE EACH EYE INDEPENDENTLY.

This one is downright weird. Imagine being able to look in two different directions at the same time?! How cool would that be? The outstanding ability of the seahorse to look in multiple directions at once helps it find food faster *and* look out for predators. It's superpower vision at its best!

SEAHORSES ARE THE UNDERWATER SUPERHEROES THE OCEAN NEEDS.

Seahorses help keep marine ecosystems healthy and thriving by hoovering the seabed, coral reefs, and mangroves of potentially harmful tiny creatures. They are the ocean's vacuum cleaners! By controlling the numbers of tiny animals in coral reefs, seagrass beds, and mangroves, seahorses help make sure their ocean home stays balanced and beautiful for everyone who lives there.

SEAHORSES CAN TRAVEL FAR AND WIDE...BY HITCHHIKING!

Although most seahorse species tend to stay close to their native habitat, some have been known to travel great distances by hitchhiking on floating seaweed.

SEAHORSES HAVE NO TEETH AND NO STOMACH. THEY MUST EAT NON-STOP.

The snout of a seahorse is an efficient vacuum tool that takes food out of the water and straight into the intestine. Without a stomach to store food, this incredible animal must constantly eat to stay alive. An adult seahorse will feed up to 50 times in a single day!

SEAHORSES COMMUNICATE BY DANCING AND MAKING CLICKING SOUNDS.

Seahorses produce clicking and popping sounds, especially during feeding and courtship. These sounds are made by rubbing parts of their skull together, a behavior known as "**stridulation**." As an FYI: this is the same method used by grasshop-

pers and crickets to make their sounds! Stridulation is a way for seahorses to communicate with each other. This fascinating ability shows that even though seahorses are small and quiet, they are very complex creatures! Yet the most famous way seahorses communicate is through dance, something they do with their partners at the beginning and throughout the courtship ritual, which can last for several days.

THERE MAY BE MANY MORE SEAHORSE SPECIES WE HAVE YET TO DISCOVER.

The pesky thing about being such a good camouflage expert is that you can also go undetected by marine biologists. Scientists have discovered over a dozen new seahorse species in just the last 20 years alone! This means there may be many more species of seahorses out there who are *so good at hiding* that we have yet to discover them.

And isn't that a super exciting thing to know?

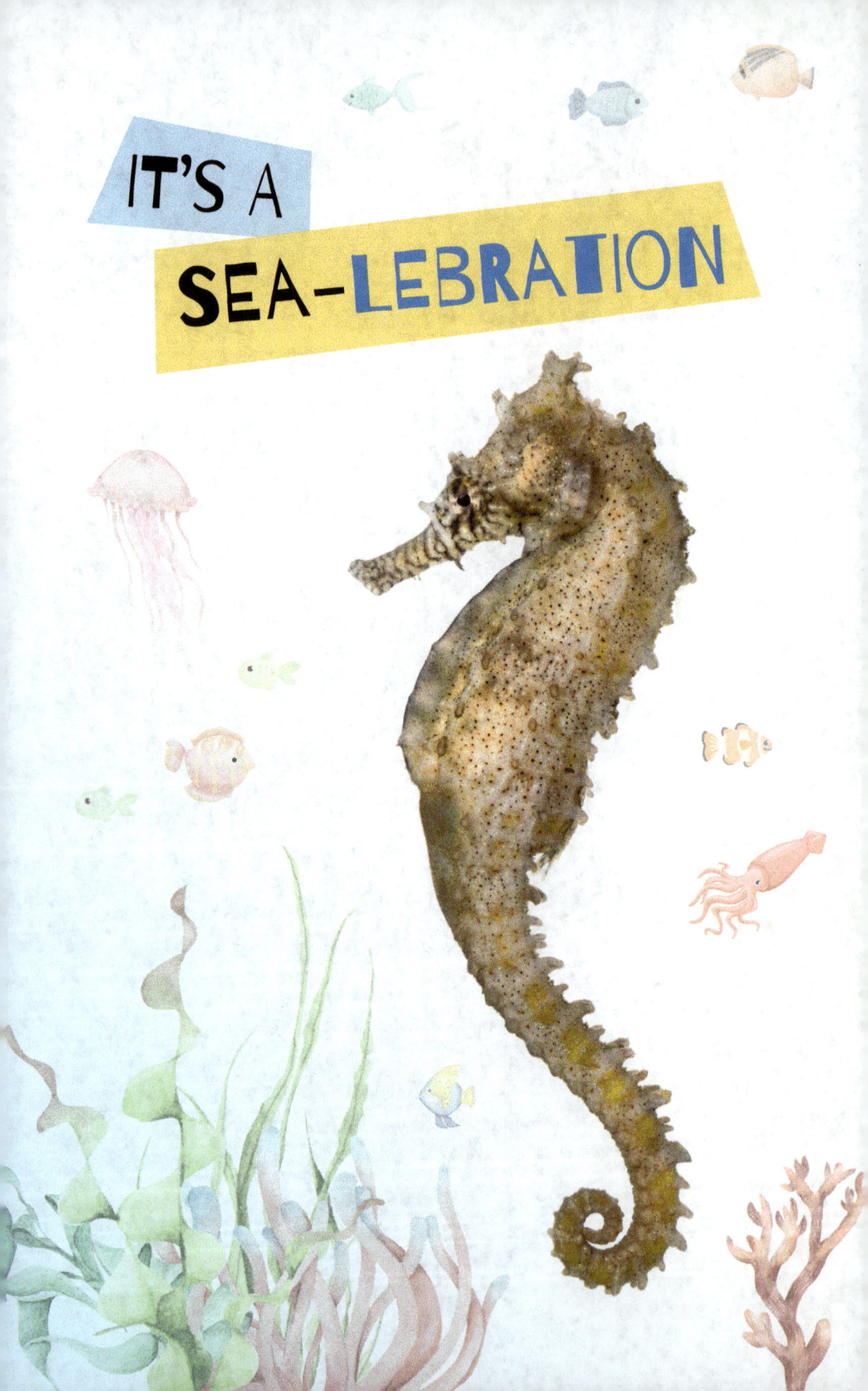

YOU'RE A SEAHORSE PRO!

Congratulations, Seahorse Smarty Pants! You've learned all about seahorses. From their habitats and diet to their lifecycle and unique traits, you are now a true seahorse expert!

By exploring the mysterious underwater world of these extraordinary creatures, we hope you will be inspired to learn even more about the animal world. Remember to share your knowledge with family and friends!

Imagine how impressed they will be when you tell them that male seahorses give birth or how seahorses can move each of their eyes independently. You can explain why they cling to seaweed with their tails and how they change color to hide from predators. You have become a real seahorse smarty pants, and that's a fantastic achievement you can be proud of!

Thank you for taking the time to read our little book from beginning to end! We hope you enjoyed learning about these incredible creatures as much

as we enjoyed sharing their story with you. The underwater world is full of wonders, and there are always more amazing animals to discover.

Keep exploring the wonderful world of animals! Whether it's seahorses, dolphins, or butterflies, every creature has its unique story, and there's always something new to learn. So, keep your curiosity alive and continue diving into nature's fascinating world.

So, here's to you, the newest seahorse expert! Keep swimming through your adventures, and remember, the world is full of exciting discoveries just waiting for you.

Great job, and happy exploring!

THANK YOU!

Thank you for reading this book and for allowing us to share our love for seahorses with you!

If you've enjoyed this book, please let us know by leaving a rating and a brief review wherever you made your purchase! This helps us spread the word to other readers!

Thank you for your time, and have an awesome day!

For more information, please visit:
www.animalreads.com

© Copyright 2025 — All rights reserved Admore Publishing

ISBN: 978-3-96772-176-8

ISBN: 978-3-96772-177-5

ISBN: 978-3-96772-178-2

Animal Reads at www.animalreads.com

The content contained within this book may not be reproduced, duplicated or transmitted without direct written permission from the author or the publisher.

Under no circumstances will any blame or legal responsibility be held against the publisher, or author, for any damages, reparation, or monetary loss due to the information contained within this book. Either directly or indirectly.

Published by Admore Publishing: Gotenstraße, Berlin, Germany

www.admorepublishing.com

www.ingramcontent.com/pod-product-compliance
Lightning Source LLC
LaVergne TN
LVHW020139080526
838202LV00048B/3976